Things I Learned the Hard Way

poems

Esteban Colon

Plain View Press
http://plainviewpress.net

1011 W. 34th Steet, Ste 260
Austin, TX 78705

ISBN: 978-1-891386-10-7
Library of Congress Control Number: 2013952025

Cover photos by Lisa Komes (2013) used with permission
Cover design by Pam Knight

Acknowledgments

Gratitude to the publications that first published these poems:

"Hellos" and "Premature" in *Avatar Review*

"Perspective" in *Rhino*

"Beyond Blinds" in *Poised in Flight Anthology*

"Judging the Miss Universe Pageant" in *Point Break Anthology*

"Firearm Philosophy" in *CC&D Magazine* and *Exact Change Only*

"Frank, On Nancy" in *Edgar Avenue*

"Plain as the Nose on Your Face" in *After Hours*

"Blacksmith" in *Between Blue Lines*

"I Almost Petted Symbolism" in *Switched-on Gutenberg*

For my mother who has always supported me,

and The Great Appreciator

Contents

A Concise List of Things I Learned the Hard Way

A Concise List of Things I Learned the Hard Way   9
Don't Play Gay Chicken with a Man Who's Attracted to You   10
Don't Play Straight Chicken with Your Best Friend's Girl   12
Why Poets Shouldn't Date   14
Yes, I Love You   15
Burnt   16
Waiting for Fires to Come to Me   17
On Want   18
Relapse   19
Samsara   20
Fresh Air   22
Forevers   23
The Distance Between   26
Hellos   27
The Second Time Around   28
Before His Wife Shed Skin   30
Pre-Winter   32
Last Fall   33
May 2011   34

Perspectives

Perspective   41
Destiny   42
I Almost Petted Symbolism   43
Alone   44
Remembering Norm   45
Little Tony   46
Commute   47
Cursive Round Smooth Glass   48
On Strength   49
Brutal in these suburbs   50
Beyond Blinds   51
South Suburbs   53
Dr. Agnew   54
Young Red Head   55

In Dark Hours   56

Pleased to Meet You . . .   57

Judging the Miss Universe Pageant   58

Small Talk   59

Lesbian's Morning   60

Holding You   61

English Major's Love Poem   62

3 Poems: Undivided   63

Free Trade   64

Firearm Philosophy   65

Word Hustler   66

Frank, on Nancy   68

Reflecting Divinity   71

Touch

Touch   75

Premature   82

Got Away   83

Tranquility   84

You   86

First Love   87

Second Love   88

Sharing a cab   89

Laundromat Blues   90

After the Paramedics Arrived   92

Plain as the Nose on Your Face   93

Binge and Purge   94

I Don't Like Ceiling Fans Anymore   95

Washing Tears Away   97

Blacksmith   98

925   99

Swimming Pool Eyes   100

Small Caskets   101

Childhood Friends   102

Found Half-Gone   103

Family Business   104

The Only Question Is When   106

About the Author   107

A Concise List of Things I Learned the Hard Way

A Concise List of Things I Learned the Hard Way

1. Don't play gay chicken with a gay man who's attracted to you
2. Don't play straight chicken with your best friend's girl
3. No matter how cool you are as friends,

    Don't ever go to a wedding with someone you've honestly considered marrying.
4. No one understands you completely.

    No one.
5. Don't piss off a Latina without having

    A) a really good apology

      or

    B) someplace to move to where no one knows you
6. No one is completely alone.

    No one.
7. What women say they want

    and what they actually want

      are seldom related
8. Waiting for someone to address their issue with you is the equivalent of waiting for a nearby house fire to reach your home before trying to put it out.
9. A good idea is just a dream diary unless you're willing to put in the work to make it real
10. Nothing . . .

    nothing . . .

    nothing ever ends, it just becomes part of whatever's next . . .

Don't Play Gay Chicken with a Man Who's Attracted to You

He

grabbed my ass and it seemed a simple stab at humor as built upon years of homophobic teenagers growing up in a land before political correctness taught teens that gay was something other than an insult lobbed at someone for not displaying the proper amount of masculinity who thus felt the need to either beat anything either remotely homo erotic into the earth, or mimic such behavior in order to create a parody they could eventually grow comfortable with.

I

being part of the latter, turned back towards him and smiled, completely unaware that I was having my first encounter with someone who was honestly interested in me as a member of the same gender, assuming that this was just another round of gay chicken, rather than me being an awful but unknowing tease for someone who had to be careful with the simple act of expressing his own sexuality which I was unfortunately able to relate to simply by surrounding myself with people who were horrified by the thought of me having a sexuality without care as to how it expressed itself.

He

seemed a bit timid to play which made little sense to me considering the point was to reach for absurdity, missing the actual point until his nose broke my personal space bubble, and things became truly uncomfortable

I

looked at him slightly confused, trying to decide what was more important, sticking to my guns just long enough to let him veer away before venturing into the foothills of homosexuality, or declaring my straightness for the world to see

and

born stubborn, I couldn't step back from a challenge no matter how inane without it either doing serious harm to my body, or morality, so I waited for him to step down, to stop lips from meeting.

He
closed his eyes and leaned in.

I
reared back, feeling outmatched, stepped to the side congratulating him on
his victory with dagger words like,
"Holy shit dude, I thought you were actually going to fucking kiss me"

He
was supposed to laugh before we went out looking for some bum willing
to buy us some alcohol so we could spend the rest of the night drunkenly
talking about women and debating about the nature of a world we had seen
way too little of.

I
saw him years later for the first time since that night, asked him why he fell
of the face of the Earth.

He
kept walking. Hand in hand with his beloved, thinking me one of those
assholes who would be giving him a hard time, had I the crowd to know that
it wouldn't be my ass getting kicked.

I
watched them walking away. Wishing I had someone to walk with like that,
that I wasn't an unknowing ass, that there was any way in the world to explain,
that had I actually known what was going on, we would've just skipped the
damn game, and went right into drinking and talking

. . .

like the friends,
I still wish we were.

Don't Play Straight Chicken with Your Best Friend's Girl

He
cried philosophy from behind brown eyes, listened
to her coo'

assumed
abandon, fueled by liquor would
lead like musicians on drugs to
new levels of understanding, the unspoken assumption of those who haven't
that
those who have
know something
they don't.

He
put together spare parts, attempting to reanimate
lost time with
all the things he assumed should have been
in the patchwork of his past.

assumed
those who rode with him, did so out of desire
and not other things,
like curiosity,
self-loathing,
a desperate hope
that their presence could deter his intentions

He
stared back at me from the mirror with
a stranger's mouth, wrapped around his penis,
crying
at his horrible luck.

assumed
the wedding ring in his sock drawer
a mistaken purchase
her body's betrayals of pleasures,
he couldn't provide
as she silently
wished
for him.

Why Poets Shouldn't Date

     I
fell for your words
       you
fell for mine
       and
between words and flesh lay reality
        where
neither of us
were ready
for the other.

Yes, I Love You

You're
the tub of ice cream who arrives when I'm cold,
the opportunity knocking
when there's soap still in my eyes,
and
as you slink away
convinced
I don't want you, I
become mad enough
to strangle the doubt
straight out of your throat.

Burnt

he sings cinders
ashes
flowing from cuts in chest,
carved
from the inside

          out

Waiting for Fires to Come to Me

I
waited like a mother watching war footage clutching her son's picture.
a husband watching the hostage negotiator walk into the bank while
nervously caressing his wedding band
for
the first fight. let
my body rock under emotions sharp enough to tear skin.

I
learned

waited
like a truancy officer at the child's favorite field, like
a paid detective at the hotel they rented every Thursday, ready to take photo
evidence for their spouses,
for
your words like curtains
drawn back,
ready
for whatever was to come.
assumed
an easy answer past was a map of time

I
learned
. . .
of the ashes after fire
. . .
I learned.

On Want

you looked at me amused.
assuring me that you weren't interested in the blues man roughly your
father's age.
He was just interesting.

I looked at you concerned.
assuring you that I wasn't interested in the nineteen year old girl who hung
around all the time
She was just interesting.

and

watching time call us both liars
way
after the fact, I
can't help but catalog
many of the things we were wrong about back then.
wondering,
how blind we still are.

Relapse

Wheels turn
tires slowing to a crawl, as
time runs low on batteries
falling so far back, the
seconds forget how to tick
my
face pressed to the window
seeing lost days knock,
come
back to the present, but
not to me, and
my,
chest forms knots
imagining seeing her, and
what I'd try to say
shrinking in her sight
lost in her smile,
and I've
lost so much time over her loss, I
can't imagine how she'd react
dreaming of
the polite disgust I expect, and as
wheels turn,
time slowing to a crawl, I
keep on driving
falling so far back into the day
I almost forget time slowed
ignoring
the tears
trying to ruin my song

Samsara

before she pumped her fists,
she
broke things
explored
every inch of home
as her mother
dutifully
picked up the pieces

before she owned her home,
she
broke things
smashed uncaring monoliths
despite arrests,
skinned knees
till her flesh and blood peers,
ceased
being cogs

before her daughter, her home
was a glorified mirror
reflecting the woman she wished to be
wouldn't
make messes
she didn't want to clean

before her daughter could walk,
she
learned to change diapers
kiss

boo boos
create a home safe to explore,
watch messes
being made
before dutifully
        picking up the pieces

      before her daughter settled down,
she
waited up at night,
posted bail
watched her little girl skin knees
trying to break monoliths
as she watched messes made
dutifully waiting
        to pick up the pieces

Fresh Air

I don't think about the way my feet push off the ground inside my running shoes as I burn calories on empty streets

I don't think about the looks trying to pull my ears away from ear buds as old songs keep my blood pumping faster

I don't think about the wind trying to dig into bones as trees open arms to reveal thousands of green children waiting for clouds to weep

I don't think about the way a poem wraps around your body, my pen charging my body till I'm the dog left at home bounding off furniture when the right words finally open the door

I don't think about grinding teeth, the ears my words fall out of despite sharp skills that have cleaned messes for too many years

I don't think about how how wide my mouth can smile when it is just me and the sun and my legs pumping away

I don't think
when I run

I don't think
when I run

I don't think
when I run

Forevers

    Young
fingers nervously touched her back,
her
outlet spine
lightening
fingertips full
of caffeinated nerves
begging
for permission
to wrap around
her rear,
mind,
too caught in the moment to imagine a desire beyond that.

    Young
eyes looked away
lashes bouncing
waiting
to be chased,
his
matchstick fingers
touched the
wet gasoline of her back
her
denial of his whims
a
moral trapping
as easily removed as her blouse

    Young
lips spoke in awkward fragments
trying
to talk the Teflon
that leads to
meeting mouths

Esteban Colon

      Old
hand touches her back,
each
finger charged with a different memory
except for the longest two,
who
share a smile,
share
intimate knowledge of her scent
tethered
to nostalgia's grin
an
uncomfortable present.

      Old
hand touches her back,
each
finger a divine leech
teeth
in her spine
suckling anxiety
palm
a valentine
sharing his intentions
as words never could.

      Old
fingers
touch their lips
treasure chests
holding memories
of sweat and screams,
who she
is,
who she
was,
uncomfortable in this shared moment
left and
right ventricles
disagreeing on who to beat for, she
introduces
the only men who've ever mattered
to each other.

      Young
fingers entwine
mimicking post coital legs
softly
promising forevers
they'll take decades
learning to understand.

The Distance Between

Not
brave enough
for vulnerability,
he collapsed
into strength

Hellos

I'm
just old enough to know how
time is fluid,
Lake Michigan in Chicago winds, slapping the coast
like
a wayward daughter,
unrepentant in her defiance,

crests,
jagged like
serrated blades cutting sky
and

I'm just old enough
to know how quickly time flows
so forgive me
if I need to hold you
a bit longer.

The Second Time Around

Pimples smoke adult cool,
young lips pour liquid death into the air, as she,
serpentine
coils round a face she loves to watch, a
DaVinci in flesh,
demure canvas framed in dark hair,
rubenesque model in modern trimmings, circled as
a split tongue licks her pheromones from the remains of her eyes,
carrying scent with clouds and sun, till
words circle like rings of smoke
curled against her ears
gaze falling into Lucifer's grin,
leaving his lips like clouds,
smile watering seeds,
blinding eyes to
the tan line round his finger, as
minds joined hands
strolling across words like warm sands
as decades
as ephemeral as smoke flee his memory,
inner eyes reborn in youth's flame,
burning bridges and trappings like cicada husks
crumbling as they're brushed away,
like the broken hearts of his children,
as together,
time resurrects snow globe memories
folding themselves till,
every moment bears a Polaroid sun,
illuminating the world he printed in greyscale,
before his wife shed skin,
washing scars clean with a new face
reincarnated

before she stopped breathing,
his heartbeats,
tribal drums played with hummingbird wings,
rising in patterns like spider webs,
replacing lusts 4/4, as
wolverine minded,
he thrashes wildly,
caught
in the quicksand sweet words
he once watered for her

Before His Wife Shed Skin

The Second Time Around pt.2

    Nipples rise, stones in cold
dreaming murder as pursed lips inhale death,
liquid
released into air, the
lover of winds she once was,
sun dress spins stored in
clenched eyes who
catalog memory,
remind petite granite fingers how
diamonds once blinded eyes, once
lacked chain to straying heart, the
wandering gaze once addicted to her
form
held for seed's stability, the
stopwatch lives of children, blink of
time/endurance
before shedding snake skin, holding
shattered promises
sun-bleached memories,
  . . .

    synapses rest,
crazed squirrels preparing for winter
measured in age, her
youngest's ascent to adulthood, as
soft skin endures the insults, her
assumed ignorance of his
indiscretions
as
smooth marble hands hold walls on their home
intact 'til,

children leave nest,
cigarette butt husband exhausted,
flicked to earth, refuse,
he chose to be, as
stronger than that, she turns
returning to life

Pre-Winter

Like Blues on a School Night

   Déjà vu blooms
with
roots in textbooks and debauchery,
leaves
reaching for sky
asking the clouds to rain Old Fashioned, or
whatever cheap liquors demand audience this day, and
sandwiched between buildings on a deck like cleavage, I
don't know anyone anymore
don't know
myself anymore, but
I do know my life, what
comes after the next sunrise
the next day when
leaves rot, shrinking
like a dead violet, like
a living metaphor
for a life
I can only pretend to live.

Things I've Learned the Hard Way

Last Fall

       Brown leaves grew dizzy
twisting naked through dead air
outside solid walls where
salt and alcohol mixed,
smoke
wafting like exhaled spirits
filling tired livers
in
willow tree branches
bent over bars, bleeding stories like stab wounds, till
covered in leaves, they burn past with
liquid flames
ignited
in the backs of throats
as
transplanted, their
roots curl
outstretched hands becoming weak fists
unable to hold on to anything
save bittersweet ghosts,
with claws in arteries.

Function

ality

reality

banality

The clenched eyes of one hundred conspiracy theorists open portals to our
own dimension

When

things are bleak enough people shut off their brains

turn

to fake explosions or love stories or whatever it is that doesn't reflect the
spinning blue pearl

whipping past sun like past glories

sunspot streaming out

spitting straight into faces

trickling down

No one

understands economics who isn't getting paid to understand economics

No one

getting paid to understand economics should be trusted by those with
enough money to be stolen

endings allow us to fabricate meaning/

structure/

allow us to . . .

create dictionaries for the unspoken/unknowable

breathe deep sighs of children so deep in trouble it doesn't matter how late
they are or when the finally manage to make it home, because the world
has already scheduled them for the worst it has and thus actions no longer
have consequences . . .

it's apocalypsariffic!

dangle thread resources thinning, he
looks for understanding
looks for understanding
looks for understanding.
                    two job tired had
          eyes searching for lower brain functions, had
        eyes searching for things that sing to throbbing mind,
             rub shoulders like imagined wife
seeing the faces of characters from a show we frequently watch affects the
             mind the same way that encountering friends does.
                        the same way
                  just like chocolate . . .
                        and love

          . . .

                                 I
love . . .
        thinking about you
                    searching for a mirror
                justification outside of self
                        self checking
                     reality checking
no longer accepting the data from senses to be the end all and be all of the
             cosmic structure encircling supposed limbs
                     supposed limbs
                     supposed limbs
        arms flailing in the night as a turning form looks for rest
      arms working deep into the night as forms beg for rest
arms idle into the night, flailing around looking for meaning
looking to be included in the dialog the
narrative with the rest

          . . .

                  tangible good marked worth
                   work good make worth

lose worth with work

make out like a pretty girl on Valentine's day with an ugly stranger since
she's too scared of being alone at the checkpoints.

we're all

alone at the checkpoints

can't

seem to find all the pieces necessary to escape the gravity of checkpoints,

sans

age.

age is

wrinkle skin/bald head/white hair/bad back/stiff hips/unhip march towards
death

is

an enemy combatant,

arm yourself.

arm yourself.

arm yourself.

soft hands young hands

hard hands old hands

soft hands young hands,

hard hands old hands

soft

hands never scraped on ground

no visible scars

never caught skin on the

blade of a knife/ piece of concrete/ side of someone's face/ shattering
mirror/ glass

lies

without function

lies

about function

lies

Things I've Learned the Hard Way

                                    still,

dangle thread marionettes look for purpose/
          function
                    ality
look for
splinters of self/
look for
          ease.
          The clenched eyes of a lonely planet wish for connection without
openness, reality without misery for a reality that need not be checked.

                              infants
               don't know to fear gravity until they fall
                              would
               fly without the eyes of parents, the fears ever-present.
                         they'd fly.

We
lie to ourselves.
                    everyday
                                   everyday
                                             everyday

                                                       waiting,

for someone to call our bluff

Perspectives

Perspective

1. *After Building Snow Forts, the boy comes inside*

    Cold touch, icicles
wrapped in flesh, just
warm enough not to freeze water
polar
opposite heat
emanating from furnace
open
      flame.

    He
sees them approach,
wrap
arms around him,

             smiling

2. *Final memories from Aushwitz*

    Cold touch, icicles
wrapped in flesh, just
warm enough not to freeze water
polar
opposite heat
emanating from furnace
open
      flame.

    He
sees them approach,
wrap
arms around him,

             smiling

Destiny

words,
arranged,
existing,
placed in order
find hands to fulfill
prophecies pre-written
similarities
to persons/things
there already, a
forgone
conclu-
sion

I Almost Petted Symbolism

He stood so close we could have kissed,
and
as that realization startled us both, I
started walking away
hoping never to
be on the business end of his antlers, he
not wanting to die on a simple morning meant for grazing, and
as he moved forward
I moved forward
six feet stopping at once, and
in that moment I knew,
his torso
was chained to my belly button,
today
he was born from my eyelids
breathing
through my existence, and
as long as I needed to rest eyes upon him
he was there,
tearing the dark out of soul, till
tears manufactured by morning
bore fruit and trees, and
as my slow mind finally rang the Bell curve,
feet
walked on,
he disappeared
and smiled an abstraction
just like the face
of the blink which bore him.

Alone

      Time tears into small shoulders, as
naked,
he lies,
curled into himself,
lungs heavily forcing air in, as
his body almost smiles in its absence,
eyes clenched so tightly
he can almost forget he exists

Things I've Learned the Hard Way

Remembering Norm

      Hephaestus verse
flows like alchemy,
liquid gold,
stretching
beyond the shallow limitations
of third eyes,
wand touched seas, the
Platonic form of rhyme.

      His
slide-show sonnets gave
inspiration dimensions,
cooled stars,
long enough
to let small hands
touch
the cosmos

Little Tony

Like a lover ignored, she
curls by the phone,
television
doing its best impersonation of company, trying to
hypnotize strong eyes with
sickly blues and reds, flickering with
the attention flesh forgot,
her mind folds slowly,
preferring instead to
hear past memories, to
read each
turn, fold and bump previously laid
. . .
        she,
waits in the wings like an understudy
reciting lines,
living as if to pass time,
till children like bees, stop long enough to hear her tears,
'til
the silence of her home
buzzes too loud for sanity

Commute

sometimes I dream of disasters
lazy eyes staring out the window as my imagination slows down that taxi,
by less than a second,
introduces doubt into his mind before he cuts us off, and
instantly gravity shifts.
The world slows.
slide-show moments, as
idle chatter turns to screams, the
airborne bus making right/down
whilst my eyes drink shakes of broken glass
peers
falling from sky into street, as
signs fly through windows, still turning
world
spinning, as
I fly up,
out of my seat,
arm still sore from hitting side, trying to
remember to move enough so
neck wont snap, and
as she skids
bus
squealing to a stop,
we look around at the broken and bloody
begging God none have died, too
scared
to find out ourselves, I hobble out,
looking for help, till my eyes
return to the now,
staring at passing lights
dreaming
of disasters.

Cursive Round Smooth Glass

The woman danced
cursive round smooth glass
frothing top erupting alcohol
dropping like campfire ashes
upon spaghetti straps under
a tidal wave,
caught
by wind like the moon
her
hand tightened
intertwined fingers
spiraling with friends
orbiting a
golden loss of inhibition
in a
small
red
dress

On Strength

Like the phoenix,
you rise
showing black suits
how to move on
before returning to your coffin

Brutal in these suburbs

Yowling cats prove evolution,
no
longer staring out kitchen windows
or gossiping
through phones

Beyond Blinds

Two tone leaves spasm in
seizure winds
limbs
rocking, bending
at nigh impossible angles.

Wind.
like a Gemini cat reaches
paws into bushes,
bats
around airborne plastic bags,
purrs
crowd surfing over a
thousand blades of grass, a
green ocean near night
complete
with waves,

                     and rising tides.

Birds,
like children dragged through grocery stores are
the first to
break the frame,
run
feathers through paint,
smearing
small sections of tapestry
bravely
paving the way for
the occasional sedan, or
minivan who
sits
pregnant
at the bottom edge, till

Esteban Colon

51

silent screams ignite, as she
opens
reveals
children trapped inside, exploding out the
waters of a river
squeezing
through a quarter sized hole in the damn
while
a full grown woman
emerges more slowly from the front,
mouth a
third hand, kicks
the door shut, nucleus
for her
well-trained electron children, swirling
cloud
lapping round her till
the edges of brick, house
like a mountain on the horizon
obscures her from vision,
makes her
cease
to exist.

Sound
politely asks glass
patio doors for admission
stays
still as
sun-bleached chairs
whispering
at the edges
through beaks.

Things I've Learned the Hard Way

South Suburbs

A block away
.38 calibers of bullet
tore through an eight year old's chest,
body
seizing in the air
exploding heart the
sudden pop of a balloon
staining grass behind her, where
an overturned bicycle
joins with homes
who still hold on to illusions of suburbia.

Dr. Agnew

Minimalistic face, her
ears hear the function of machines, world a
cool gray,
opposite of
the chaos she clutched in youth, the
aspect of sun who
bleaches canvas,
burns color through brightness, refining intellect, till
tongue turns
youth's idealism to confetti, aging
quickly under skin, as
minimalist face, her
titanium flesh
remains pristine, riding
a core of ice

Young Red Head

       Apple sat, whirled
spun
like Rumpelstiltskin thread
before
Exxon spill eyes
un-
       able to
lay gaze upon anything without
molasses mud filling every orifice
smiling
before Playboy leers,
as
well to do men
cheapen themselves
for the honor
of a moment's
attention

In Dark Hours

smaller than
one
would have thought, curious
fingers trace edges. Run
track meet skin 'round contours,
till
taskmaster brain cracks whip.
fingers push
tiny headstones into chambers,
where they excitedly wait
to mine blood.

Pleased to Meet You . . .

His pristine tongue weaves words
aged like wine till perfect,
he reaches down his hand

pulling unformed talent
forward with whispered words
molding a young man's path

before he disappeared
lost to the memories
of gray matter mythos

and in the vacuum, his
prodigy resets bones
redefining his face

molding furious words
his stained young hands, create
art, begging to be cooled

chaos with four corners
reflecting the divine
in everyday people

Judging the Miss Universe Pageant

fingers
still membrane slick, she changes color,
                strangers rattle,
bodies like air dancers
        blessed with the power to moan in ecstasy
we
all voted after that,
knew the rest of the events were a sham
dared not make eye contact till the break
where we all
changed our pants.

Small Talk

stairway wit banter left
half smiles
staring at feet
riding
staccato laughter as
butterfly stomaches
begged
former strangers
stay

Lesbian's Morning

        I understand that under skin, you can feel my waist curve,
luscious breasts curl up to you, but
despite smiles that beg your lips to shut them up, I'm
still male, and
you left in a robe over five minutes ago . . .
        by now I expect you walking through the house
areolas catching the light of
small bulbs shaped like flames,
reaching for your second cup of coffee, while
my early morning erection is
birthed from dress pants tying material to your ass
like a ribbon in case I could somehow forget, but
you're still in your mirror
fixing hair
(and blemishes)
that hardly need be touched, which I know
because I've just returned from there,
male legs transporting eyes
waiting for fantasy past, and
as you return to the room, my
lust has fallen asleep,
replaced by a smile,
begging
to be shut up

Things I've Learned the Hard Way

Holding You

Memories have us
balled up like
joyful yarn,
an octopus loving dumb
and useless arms

. . .

English Major's Love Poem

    I
share my life with you, and
      you
share your life with me, and
    I
dream of the day
    our
pronouns
are plural.

3 Poems: Undivided

My mind is filled with:

Eavesdropper echoes; shards; too many thoughts
sharp; to focus; hate/love/bullshit/random jokes/"didja see the look on her
face!"
false connection to loves who focus; thick enough; eyes everywhere, till
vice grips ; only to; higher functions forgotten and it

drip(s)

small thoughts

Free Trade

       I would give up every bit of rhythm
for the weight of your words
who
clutch to my heart like
nine year old faces pulled from the sea,
bloated blue by
water soaked lungs
drowned
on the tears
their eyes froze crying

Firearm Philosophy

shotguns don't get high.
shotguns
don't talk outside bars till sunrise,
stumble away,
still unsure of life paths.

shotguns
don't quiet their minds with pills
desperate
for five
       solid
hours of sleep.

shotguns live for the kill
              the smell of sulfur.

shotguns
don't ask
don't fight for peace.
they assume there is none,
and dare you
           to prove them right.

Word Hustler

He
sells Christmas from the back of his truck
keeps
bootleg reindeer in his trench coat,
speaks with
words below the handlebar,
thoughts
somewhere south of equality,
spilled like
a bucket of sand
who's echoes will live
forever
in the smallest crevices of your ears, a
liquored up linguist, he
drunkenly lets
refinery words bless minds like
champaign bottles,
falling in shards
down the hull of a ship
joys like
sunshine sickness,
just as
poisonous as
his well abused veins.

He's
a new age shaman full of
second hand sermons and
first person nightmares, an
Indian vomiting candle light poetry
to
listeners walking on their back-feet
tails tucked in disbelief
of truth from the cracks, where he
finishes Russian Roulette verse
stares at a stunned room,
holding his
gun by the barrel,
asking
                    "next."

Frank, on Nancy

I swear she'll fuck me to death,
legs
wrapped 'round my sexy grave
searching for a stiff one.

College
had us balled up, a
crumpled
paper of flesh, set to
tumble dry
cycle
moaning and screaming for hours.

Sex
couldn't wait for
          bedrooms,
          stripshows,
          condoms

                 . . .

Our
first son filled her belly,
wedding
dress fitted to hold him, her
radiant face
had heart
rushing to
conclusions my
loins made long ago.

Bills,
work hours
soccer practice
meetings
church, all
somehow found ways to
fuck the fucking,
remove
sexual intercourse from the lexicon, till
repression
grows thick enough
that newspaper ads can do it for us,
touches wane,
fear of
ripping clothes off each other in the middle of
Macy's
office parties
school plays
public pools
church, all
rest in the back of hands, who
slowly
grow too timid to touch.

She will
fuck me to death,
fill
time the kids are away with nuclear explosions of sex,
tidal
waves of orgasms,
love making never
showing up,
            till we've gotten all the

                                    fucking

out of our systems.

        We're addicts, but
how do I tell her
that in the small moments
when
touch is impossible,
when
my body must be at   work
                         business trips
                         dinner meetings
                         planning sessions,
when she's   still asleep
                hanging out with her friends
                watching the kids,
I've

found another dealer.

Reflecting Divinity

Alix Olson said
"God would be a dike
if she could find someone to hold her,"
but like
any of the seeds blown off their maker
dandelion in the wind, she
craves touch, lies
lonely at night wondering if
all the decisions that lead her here were worth it,
and I'm sure God would
curl fingertips into blankets, arching her back, were
she to meet the right woman,
just like
I'm sure she still dreams of
flesh on flesh, night
ripped in half by orgasmic screams,
and
as much as she wants to
I'm sure she sits like me
staring at the empty pillow, knowing
that no matter how much she aches for Satan
it would never work out, that
despite a shattered heart
precariously placed back together
she still smiles every sun rise
open
to whatever's next to come

Touch

Touch

4.   breasts/neck/collarbone/navel/giant eyes/lips/nipples/inner
        thighs/knees/wrists
                                under
        the bead of
        shower water
        shower
                wall
        hard enough to take the slam of our bodies
        pressing
        at a force
        atoms
        fuse or break,
        teeth -
                tracing skin unmarred
        tongues -
                craving crevices
        most
        thoughts defined by
        roving eyes.

        Desire
                so
        thick,

                                        bodies
                                        vibrate.

        we're
        out of condoms.
        will not
        stop fucking
                till sunrise.

5.   cool night fuck-fest left
                        stains on walls
                        rug-burned bodies.

Years later, closed eyes would still see
your horse trained hips
snake – rolling
arched
back galloping
behind
bouncing breasts, my
fingers curling so far inside you, your
scent
forgot to wash off,
                        hoarse
screams in my ear
                        voice
breaking with the rotation of thumb
on clitoris

finding
fifteen ways
to earn screams.

2.   cool air skin lets
     horned tongue whisper honey,
     negotiate the price

                              of your virginity
     erase
     lines you carved in stone,

                         finds
     curled bodies, your
     compliant hands
     stroking the

                    flaccidity
     out my penis

                    between your
     unpenetrated legs,

                         I
     act out
     what we both want,
     mirror
     futures not yet predicted
     before
     the first seal breaks,

                         your
     awkward mouth
     trying to inhale my tongue,

                         slowly
     trained before diving deeper,
     proving
     oral fixations easily
     overcome

                    a lack
                    of experience.

7.   Misscommunication   break
      down walls   break
      down binds   break

      futures who skipped down sunlit streets till
      attempts to stay friends,
      leaves us
                      staring
            and   speaking,

                      God

      commanding you leave me,
                                      my
      leaning
      leaving
                your breath   stuttering
                your eyes   panicking
      (lungs thick with beliefs like bullshit)
      caught
                in headlight memories
      your
                nipples
      poking through your sensible sweater.

6.   dimmer switch morality,

                           yours
turns the wrong way,
leaving me
like a rowdy inmate,

                    quickly losing privileges,
leaving me
           wondering
if God
has taken my place,
crawling into your bed at night
with greedy
trumpet boy fingers

                    and a divine penis.
    . . .

Five
       hundred miles from home,
imagination
rides matchstick fingers,
traveling
at the speed of foreplay,
panting
till   every   act

                    (sans entry/props)
lays exhausted,
staring at us like
linked
marriage vow eyes
quivering
at the magnetic pull
of the unholy.

I
bite my tongue,
         who wonders
         if anal
         is a sin

              . . .

3. Fresh bud love
    laid
                rose petal paths
    a
                freshly drawn bath,
    our
                marriage coo smiles.

    fire
    hands replaced with
    silken fingers,
    bed sheets
                        that would never wash
    pure.

    scents
                like first touches,
    your
                sweat   -   vagina sweet
    legs
                spread for the first time,
    a
                gateway drug,
    till
                junkie minded,
    you
    claw/ride/moan
                                invite
    clawing/banging,
                            a
    night we
    slam
    into one another so hard,
                                sound waves
                                rattle walls.

Things I've Learned the Hard Way

1.   Intensity
can change directions.

Head
        buried in your chest, my
Ragnarock heart
          tried to
count
each puzzle piece as they fell,
jagged
shards reflecting
days like liquor drowned memories
                              till my

redirection bed
replaced
your motherly coos
             with
grinding hips,
fingers like rakes,

             while

tiptoeing feet
curse clothes,

        all the lines

        we promised

           not to cross.

Premature

Blue she
cried so hard,
lungs burst,
and tears
fell from the eyes
of her parents

Got Away

Orpheus eyes still dream of
dark
danger, the
omnipotent allure of all women,
her
fluttering eyelids, the
span of cosmos
Izanagi and Izanami meeting,
and
Orpheus eyes still conjure her flesh,
frail
bones, clawing
with ragged nails, and
she
rises on clouds into heavens
far beyond my monkey's feet
and short
human arms

Tranquility

I'm lost,
drowning man in a sea of imperfections,
digging deeper,
floating down.
Dropping
. . .
falling
. . .
swimming,
forever looping round memories
of things I never should have thought,
never should have not done,
never . . .
never.
The mist rises,
ghostly bride of the sea
lifting away,
in one last silken caress
as the moon rises on ripples,
dancing
as silver fish dive
in and out of its glow,
My eyes are the stars
blinking in the sea,
watching
as angels swim
spiraling birds of love,
of light,
burrowing
into the back of my mind
ablaze
. . .

There is fire everywhere I see,
everywhere I look,
there is fire in the ocean
in the skies,
and I've been enjoying the splendors so long,
I forgot to breathe

You

own the soft spot
in a heart
that beats for another

First Love

I remember thinking
"nothing can stop this"
before
months passed
leaving love gasping,
gurgling through red balloons like
a street soldier
holding his neck,
in the arms of his wailing mother
signaling an ambulance,
destined
to be too late.

Second Love

Like
watching video of your own car crash, you
remember
                    vividly
how things end,
how
cloud nine doesn't pack parachutes.

It's
not like the first time when
joy is existence.
where
bliss and ignorance sew their torsos together
before dancing with you.
            This
you know.
You remember the feel of bones snapping on ground.
Sky
whipping flesh as
fragile heart seizes.

This you know.

This time,
you jump
knowing there's a ground,
simply
loving her too much to care.

Sharing a cab

      Tears have daggers in them,
each one
pouring out of eyes,
ripping into my heart, and
as you turn your head,
completely abandoned,
      I bleed
in your loneliness

Laundromat Blues

You
wanted a ring.
Never
was one for jewelry or expensive gifts.

Today, his
lazy eye reaches for my wallet,
asking
if I'd like to by the
ring his
pocketed hands
tells me he stole.

Then, I
hadn't heard any requests or revelations,
couldn't
get you to wear something we made together
on your wrist,
couldn't fathom you accepting a ring.

I
wanted to adorn you,
let
precious stones reflect diamonds permanently embedded in my eyes since
the moment I saw you,
and

. . .

Things I've Learned the Hard Way

You never told me that you
wished for a ring, and
as he
walks away,
stolen rings in my hand,
I sit
wishing
I still had you to give them to.

After the Paramedics Arrived

Winds ripped at my flesh
outside the house, signaling
herding medics in

blind uniforms move
storming through storm, or
human delusion

heavy feet reflect
fists, riding walls down stairs, my
timid feet followed

Child tucked in chest,
drowning eyes watched massive men
charge his rag-doll form

Our screams uniting
as they violently subdue
fake track-marks they "see"

minutes away from
sugarless-blood born coma
they blindly beat him.

Carcass dragged away
his diabetic dog tags
sink into the snow.

Things I've Learned the Hard Way

Plain as the Nose on Your Face

or so I thought
were my
white picket wishes, dreams of
small children curling round your legs
where I
mercilessly
tickled them half to death,
kissed
you squarely on the lips, made honest
by solid love
wrapped 'round ring finger.

Plain
as the nose on your face,
or so I thought,
was my
willingness to compromise, tear
down ancient pillars, to
rebuild together.

Plain
as the nose on your face,
was the weight of revelation
on chipped hearts
struggling,
for reasons I still don't understand,
to deny
what for a moment
we both wanted.

Esteban Colon

Binge and Purge

She
sharpened sex,
placed
samurai hands on
the handle,
sheath
drawing more blood than blade.

I Don't Like Ceiling Fans Anymore

       Spinning fan-blades remind me of hotel rooms,
someone
was always fucking in a room nearby.

In
Los Angeles, we
found ways to
travel the length of our hotel room through foreplay,
till
near the front door, we perched,
naked,
wet and erect, our
staring eyes trying to compromise
with your morality, Jesus
shaking his head, "no"
till
we collapsed,
into arm blankets,
throats
vibrating love
in tones so low,
nerves
not ears
hear it.

       Spinning fan-blades hop thoughts like
tap-dancing across the
tops of speeding cars
starts at
bedsprings squeaking
moves to
fucking ex-

girlfriends, hearing
my brother through house construction's half walls
to
the last night I spend with my girlfriend,
now
ex
. . .

      Spinning fan-blades make me want to cry,
till
a sweaty forehead ties it to
falling asleep at the sunrise,
paper, dice, books and pizza crusts, the
overpowering scent of
unwashed teens,
or
at least I try to convince myself it does
. . .

      Spinning fan-blades
make me want to cry,
each
squeak
reminding me of your smile, the
soft and playful of your kiss,
touching
skin like sun rays,
as heart
feels your absence
like an imploding star

                                                       Things I've Learned the Hard Way

Washing Tears Away

The sponge made love to nerves,
gliding along skin,
gently caressing my arm, as
you looked simply at my chest,
your touch more
comfortable than the womb warm water,
wrapped 'round our waists
the
love lines shattered several short hours earlier, and
when I
stood next to the tub, I
couldn't help but look at your pussy,
watching you
embrace the tub like the lover
I used to be, and
looking at you in there
I went a little mad,
unable to fathom not climbing in,
despite the fact that
it had only been
several bottles of wine, and
one night since you broke up with me, and
as the sun lay
infant in the sky,
we bathed each other
alone in Eden
till we got dressed
and I walked out your front door
one last time

Blacksmith

    I climbed a mountain
hoping
the man at its peak could
put
a shattered tin heart back together,
and as I rose
joy screaming about how I reached the top,
there was no man
just an anvil
a hammer
and fire.

Things I've Learned the Hard Way

925

Why I hate Chicago's electronic emergency highway signs*

numbers
are easy.

easier

> than crumpled paper steel
> fresh
> red carpet, birthed
> from cement,
> his
> unrecognizable
> crayola face.

it's easier to add 1 to the tally
than

> watching 8 year old legs
> wobble
> skin draped in red webbing,
> rocking back
> and forth
> as she cradles   her mother's stilled head.

*Chicago expressway signs show an up to date traffic related death toll tally

Swimming Pool Eyes

She had
swimming pool eyes,
flesh smooth
curves, the
ghosts in my
masturbater's mind,
shame
flooding in immediately after that thought.

She had
swimming pool eyes, and
saltwater lungs, my
cornea burning
exhausted
arms dragging her to land.

She had
swimming pool eyes,
pale skin
and
. . . I
wasn't strong enough
to pull her out, and
dry her lungs

. . .

She had
swimming pool eyes.

Things I've Learned the Hard Way

Small Caskets

At fourteen
she told me things I couldn't possibly understand,
how
the world isn't ready for her and her girlfriend,
who
with a couple of implants and a producer
would be multimillionaires,
how
I couldn't possibly understand her love
for the first person to see
naked skin,
plunge
a finger south of the equator.

At fourteen
she lashed out at my outstretched hand,
not
ready for a world
beyond roles
where skin houses people
not ideas.

At fourteen
she traced her veins for a crash
too young
to see a way out,
save
the tip
of a razor

Childhood Friends

Twenty years prior,
soft hands rose yelling
"Me! Me! Me!"

not knowing
the blue light special meant
he couldn't have it right away,
that,
paying sale prices would
string it out
over years . . .
entering his life,
like spoonfuls of dumplings at a cafeteria.

Two minutes ago leather hands rose,
palsied in pain,
thinking
back to twelve
where
curious eyes saw
death on sale
and grabbed it
tightly
between two fingers,
pinching addiction,
while he walks
like an open casket
screaming
at ghosts.

Found Half-Gone

half-closed
eyes stare into a mirror where
half-hearted
smile crosses a
half-conscious face.

half-full
arteries leak
half-way
across the floor, losing a life
half-lived.

Family Business

His mother
always hoped I'd wait longer.

She
dreaded the rising sun,
kissing
his soft pink forehead, on the day our hands met
pulling him
out of childhood.

"If you linger,
they'll become confused,
hold your leg, begging as if you made the decisions."

"I cut too slowly once,
strings
unraveling like
her body's connection to physics.
The
silence after her throat turned inside out
was worse than the screaming."

His
mother used to stare into my eyes,
dreaming
of butcher knives and cribs.
My
steady hand clearing
tears from her cheeks

"Now tighten the grip with your right hand,
just
your right hand.
The left stays loose."

Things I've Learned the Hard Way

She
always worried he'd be a quick study.
     It must have been hard to know

"Rear back,
and make sure it is one smooth motion."

"Yes!
Just like that!"

    He's
born to wield the sickle
I'd tell her I
love her
but she knows
I'm not coming home again.

The Only Question Is When

I
can't
drink and walk at the same time.

sometimes when I swallow my spit,
I
cough for about two full minutes.

Sometimes,
I
stop breathing in my sleep.

I
know
how I'm going to die.

About the Author

Esteban Colon is a writer and experiential educator from Chicago Heights. He is a founding member of the Waiting 4 the Bus Poetry Collective, the cohost of two poetry venues, and the editor of *Exact Change Only*. His works have appeared in various publications, such as *Rhino, CC&D Magazine, Avatar Review* and *After Hours*, including collections such as *Poised in Flight, Things That Go Bump in the Night, The American Open Mic. Vol. 2,* and *Point Mass*. Previous collections of his works, *Between Blue Lines*, and the poetic suite *Edgar Avenue* were released as chapbooks by Exact Change Press and Naked Mannequin Press.

CPSIA information can be obtained
at www.ICGtesting.com
Printed in the USA
BVHW04s1520240618
519716BV00002B/13/P